·VISUAL GUIDES·

TRANSPORT MACHINES

·VISUAL GUIDES·

TRANSPORT MACHINES

Norman Barrett

FRANKLIN WATTS

New York • Chicago • London • Toronto • Sydney

© 1994 Franklin Watts

Franklin Watts
95 Madison Avenue
New York, NY 10016

Library of Congress
Cataloging-in-Publication Data
Barrett, Norman S.
    Transport machines /
    Norman Barrett.
        p. cm. – (Visual guides)
    Includes index.
    ISBN 0-531-14298-1
    1. Vehicles – Juvenile
    literature.   [1. Vehicles.]
    I. Title.
    II. Series: Barrett, Norman S.
    Visual guides.
    TL147.B294 1994
    629.04'6 – dc20   93-33235
                   CIP   AC

Series Editor
Norman Barrett

Designed by
K and Co

Picture Research by
Ruth Sonntag

Photographs by
BP Oil
N.S. Barrett
Bell Helicopter Textron
French Railways
Hoverspeed
InterCity
Japan Ship Centre
David Jefferis
Muddy Fox
P & O Group
Police Department of New York
Porsche Cars
Qantas Airways
RNLI
Slingsby Engineering
Westland Helicopters

New Illustrations by
Rhoda and Robert Burns

Contents

Sports car

Sports cars are the fastest vehicles on the road. They are light and powerful. But apart from racing circuits, there are few places where sports cars can be driven at top speed because of the speed limits on public roads.

Most sports cars are built for two people, with limited space at the back for another two passengers.

▽ A Porsche 911 cruising on the road at less than half its top speed of 162 miles per hour (261 km/h).

Brake _____

_____

Front suspension – suspension reduces jolts and gives a smoother ride on uneven surfaces.

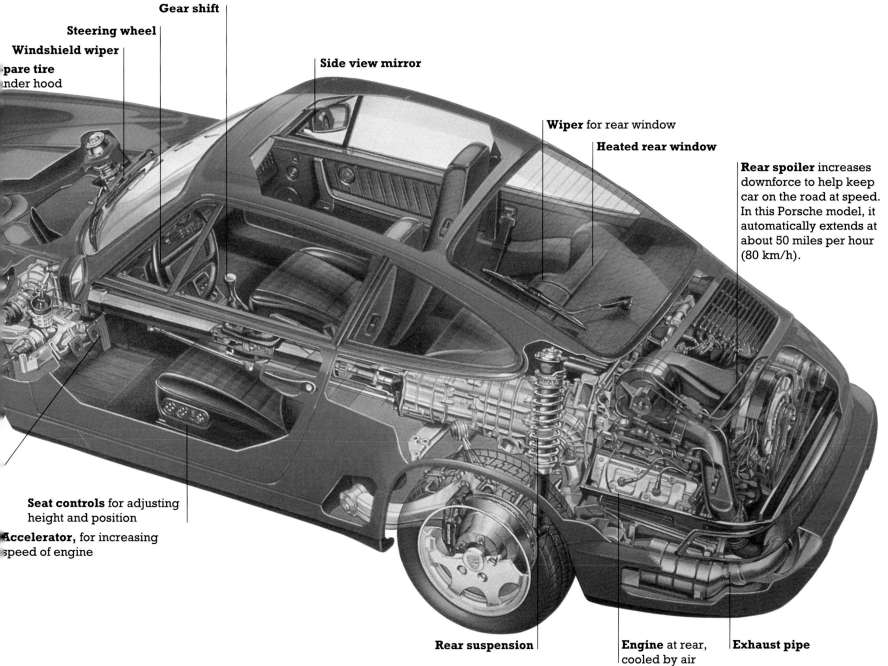

7

Gear shift

Steering wheel

Windshield wiper

Spare tire under hood

Side view mirror

Wiper for rear window

Heated rear window

Rear spoiler increases downforce to help keep car on the road at speed. In this Porsche model, it automatically extends at about 50 miles per hour (80 km/h).

Seat controls for adjusting height and position

Accelerator, for increasing speed of engine

Rear suspension

Engine at rear, cooled by air

Exhaust pipe

Windshield visor

Black-tinted glass

Extra lights fitted
into **chrome bumper**

Moon disk hubcaps

Flamed paint patter

◁ Enthusiasts enjoy
looking over custom
cars at special rallies.
Some are even for sale.
This one has an eye-
catching paint job as
well as some interesting
body changes.

Custom car

Custom cars are cars that have been altered in some way to change their appearance. People who customize their cars do so to make them different from any other car.

Customizing might just involve fancy paintwork. But sometimes interiors and engines are also customized. A car may be completely rebuilt.

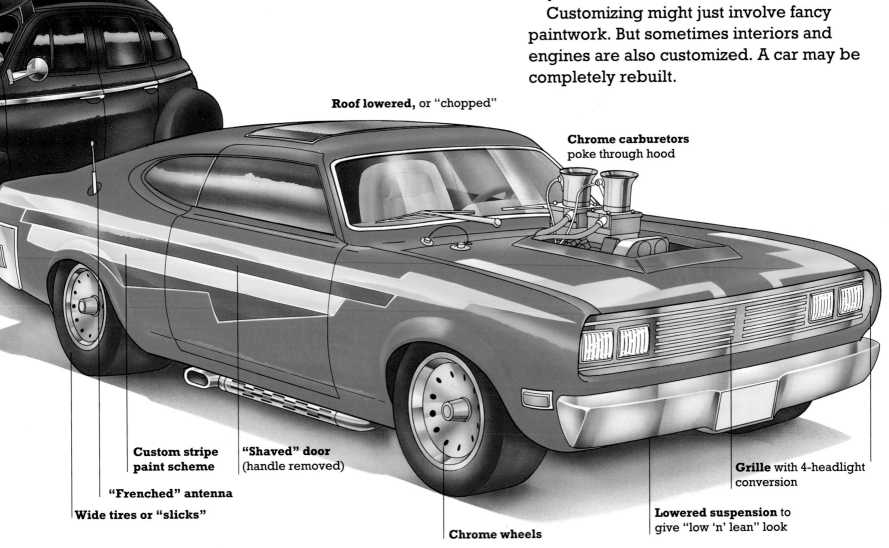

Roof lowered, or "chopped"

Chrome carburetors poke through hood

Custom stripe paint scheme

"Shaved" door (handle removed)

"Frenched" antenna

Wide tires or "slicks"

Grille with 4-headlight conversion

Lowered suspension to give "low 'n' lean" look

Chrome wheels

Supercar century

The great cars, or "supercars," are
vehicles that combine high performance
and good looks in about equal quantities.
Sadly for most people, a high price is
included, too.

The sporting supercars illustrated here
were each thought to be the tops in their
time.

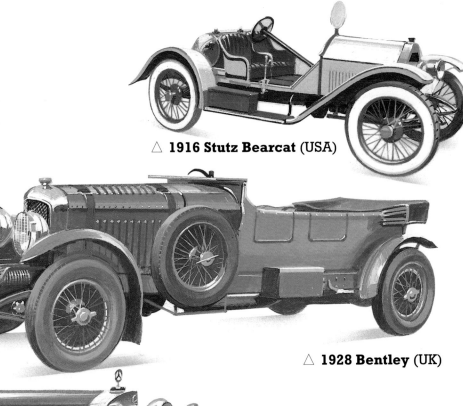

△ **1916 Stutz Bearcat** (USA)

△ **1928 Bentley** (UK)

△ **1936 Mercedes-Benz 500K Roadster** (Germany)

▷ **1947 Cisitalia 202 Coupé** (Italy)

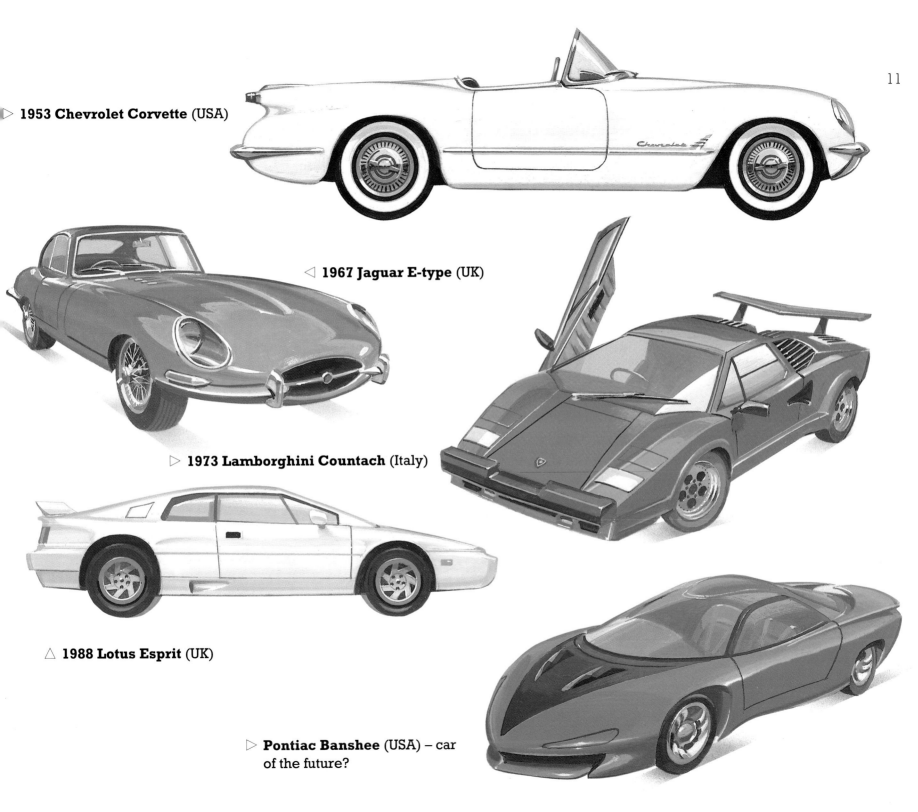

▷ **1953 Chevrolet Corvette** (USA)

◁ **1967 Jaguar E-type** (UK)

▷ **1973 Lamborghini Countach** (Italy)

△ **1988 Lotus Esprit** (UK)

▷ **Pontiac Banshee** (USA) – car of the future?

Tractor-Trailer truck

Tractor-trailer trucks are the giants of the road. They consist of a tractor unit and a semi-trailer.

The tractor unit can be driven by itself and is shown in the main illustration. The semi-trailer has no wheels at the front. It is joined to the back of the tractor unit by a coupling.

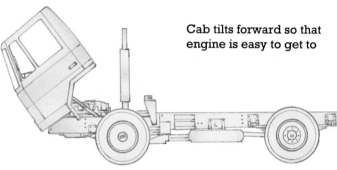

Cab tilts forward so that engine is easy to get to

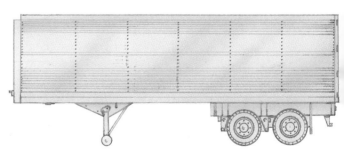

A semi-trailer has legs at the front. These are brought into use when it is not attached to the tractor unit.

◁ "King of the road." An American lumber truck with an extra trailer attached to the semi-trailer.

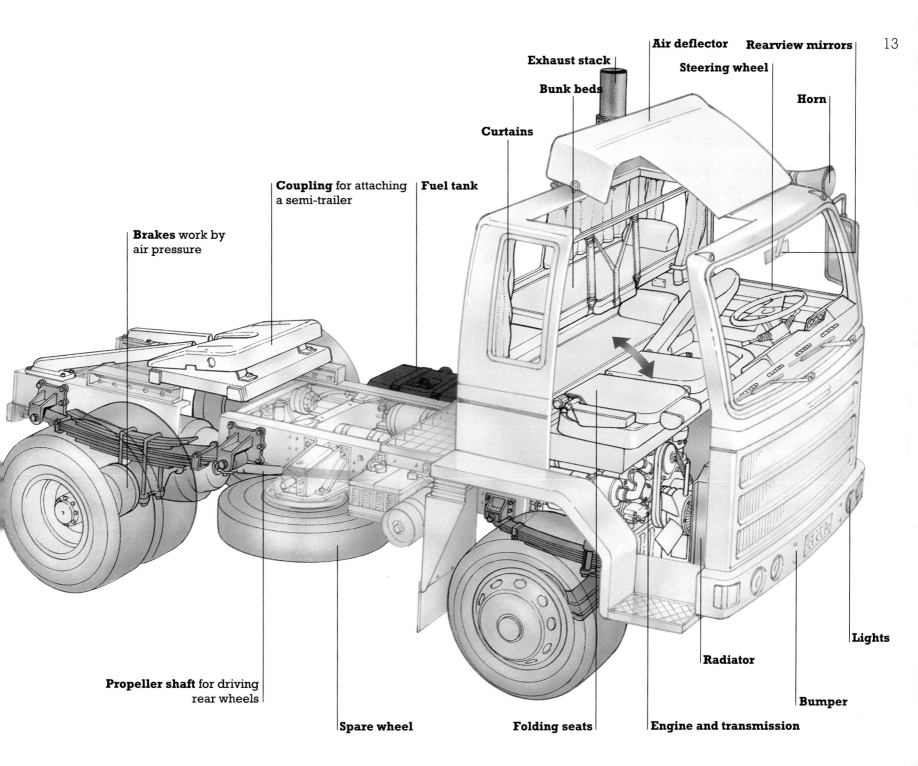

Exhaust stack

Air deflector

Rearview mirrors

Steering wheel

Horn

Bunk beds

Curtains

Coupling for attaching
a semi-trailer

Fuel tank

Brakes work by
air pressure

Propeller shaft for driving
rear wheels

Spare wheel

Folding seats

Engine and transmission

Radiator

Bumper

Lights

Trucking progress

The trucks illustrated on these pages show how they have changed from the early days of road transport to the "supertrucks" of today.

The smooth styling and streamlined shape of modern trucks is a far cry from the early models, with their starting handles and solid rubber tires.

△ **1911 Berliet** (France)

△ **1924 Thornycroft Q-type** (UK)

△ **1939 Fiat 626N** (Italy)

△ **1947 K Series International** (USA)

△ **1953 GMC** (USA)

△ **1979 Volvo F731 8x4** (Sweden)

▷ **1966 Mercedes-Benz LPS 1418** (Germany)

△ **1980s Leyland Roadtrain** (UK)   ▷ **1990s Renault AE500 Magnum** (France)

Motorcycles

◁ Motorcycles are an important means of transportation for city police. Riders can weave their way at high speeds through heavy city traffic to reach the scene of an incident.

Motorcycles are a fast means of transportation. In busy cities they can go through heavy traffic and are easier to park than cars.

The power of a motorcycle depends on the size of its engine. This is measured in cubic centimeters, or "cc." Road bikes range from about 50 to 1,000 cc or more.

Rearview mirrors

Handlebar

Clutch lever is connected to the clutch

Throttle for changing speed of engine

Brake lever works brakes

Headlight

Radiator contains water for cooling the engine of large bikes

Brake cable connects brake lever with brakes

Front forks have springs inside to smooth out the ride

Fuel tank

Passenger seat

Engine

Rider's footrest

Clutch works the gears, which transfer the power from the engine to the back wheel

Brakes slow down the wheel

Exhaust pipe takes away used gases from the engine

Chain is driven by the gears to make the back wheel go around

Rear suspension helps to give a smooth ride

Superbike century

The best "superbikes" combine high power with good brakes and superb handling. These features enable a skilled rider to go fast, but safely. Acceleration is more important than speed, so that other vehicles can be overtaken quickly.

The bikes illustrated here are rated among the best of their own time.

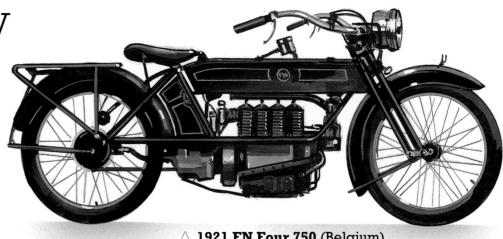

△ **1921 FN Four 750** (Belgium)

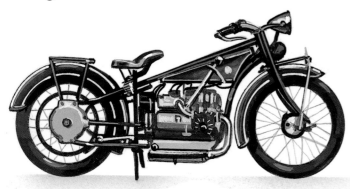

△ **1923 BMW R32** (Germany)

△ **1937 Ariel Square Four** (UK)

△ **1932 Zundapp K800** (Germany)

1968 Honda CB750 (Japan)

△ **1950s Vincent Black Shadow** (UK)

1970s Ducati 900SS (Italy)

△ **Suzuki NUDA** (Japan) – prototype bike of the near future

△ **1988 Kawasaki ZX-10** (Japan)

Touring bicycle

The modern bicycle is one of the most efficient machines ever made. It costs very little to run – no fares, fuel or tax. It does not pollute the air, and does not get stuck in traffic jams.

The classic touring machine is illustrated on the right. Mountain bikes, like the one pictured on the left, are also used for touring.

◁ The mountain bike is built for traveling over rough ground. It is constructed with strong materials and has knobby tires with deep treads for better grip on loose surfaces.

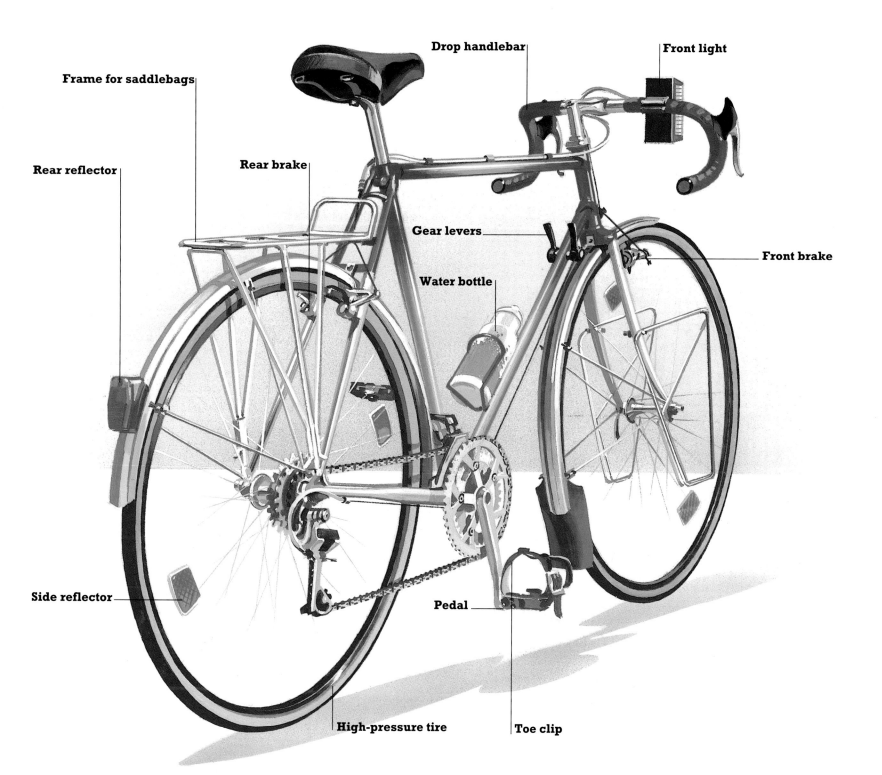

Frame for saddlebags

Drop handlebar

Front light

Rear reflector

Rear brake

Gear levers

Front brake

Water bottle

Side reflector

Pedal

High-pressure tire

Toe clip

Future bikes

Recent developments in design and the use of new materials will give future bikes a new look.

Magnesium, a very light and strong metal, is beginning to be used for frames. It allows them to be cast in one piece from molten metal – faster and cheaper than cutting and welding metal tubing.

Other modern materials include carbon fiber and various plastics, all lighter and stronger than standard tubing. Disk wheels, made of carbon fiber, are lighter than spoked wheels.

The future bike would also have waterproof brakes operated by electronic switches, puncture-resistant tires and automatic gears.

◁ This design for a future police bike includes puncture-proof tires, a siren and an equipment cylinder mounted behind the seat. Some police forces are already replacing foot patrols with mountain bikes, using them to chase criminals long after cars have had to stop – along narrow alleys or on rough ground, for example.

Year 2000 roadster

1 Side stripes glow in the dark so drivers of other vehicles can see the bike easily at night

2 Disk wheels made of carbon fiber, lighter than spokes; inside the disks are the brakes, completely waterproofed

3 Front fork is a side-mounted design, using high-strength material

4 Mini-windshield cuts air resistance, making high-speed riding easier

5 Brakes are operated by electronic handlebar switches

6 Magnesium-and-plastic frame is light and strong

7 Belt drive from pedals for smooth riding; this bike has an automatic gear system

8 Rear lighting system includes a bright braking signal

9 Puncture-resistant tires

10 Streamlined helmet has built-in radio and marker lighting

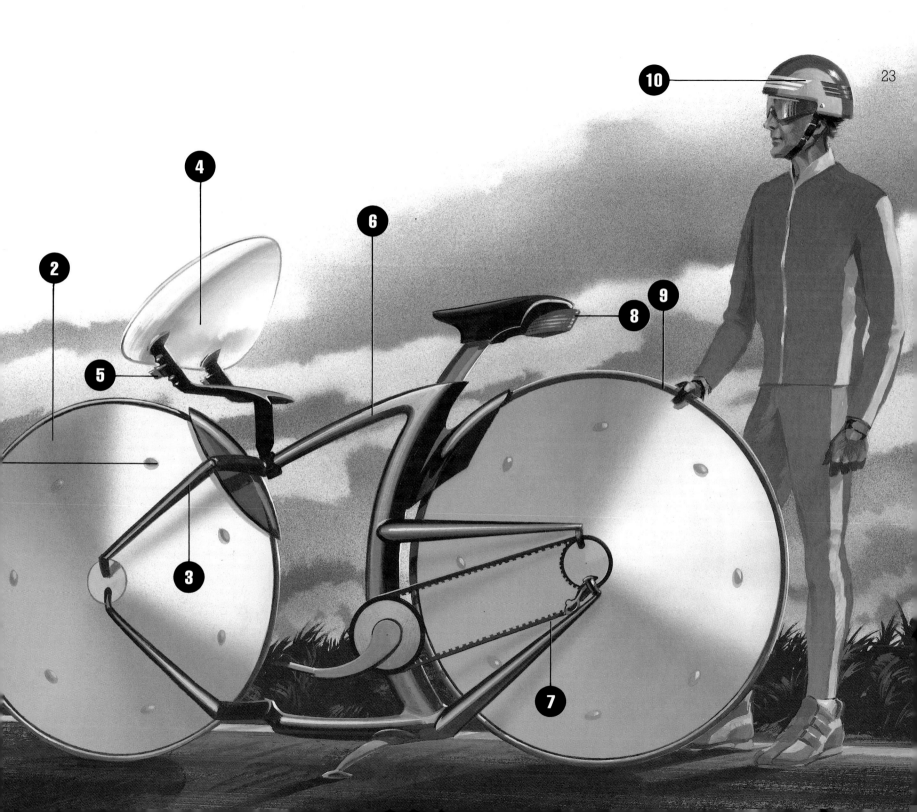

High-speed train

The fastest trains run on electricity. They receive their power from overhead wires. The power is fed to motors that turn the locomotive's driving wheels.

Electric trains reach speeds of more than 150 miles per hour (240 km/h). The locomotive pulls as many as 12 coaches, with more than 700 passengers.

◁ The high-speed train picks up its electric power from a system of overhead wires. It runs on a track with two rails.

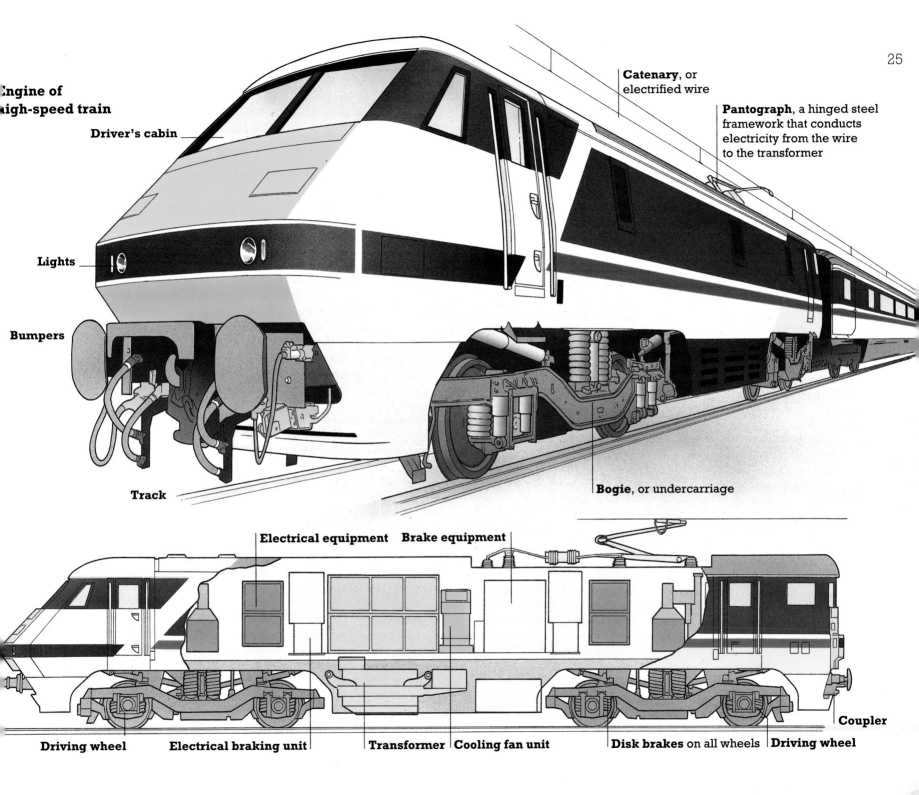

Engine of high-speed train

Driver's cabin

Catenary, or electrified wire

Pantograph, a hinged steel framework that conducts electricity from the wire to the transformer

Lights

Bumpers

Track

Bogie, or undercarriage

Electrical equipment   **Brake equipment**

Driving wheel   **Electrical braking unit**   **Transformer**   **Cooling fan unit**   **Disk brakes** on all wheels   **Driving wheel**

Coupler

Rail progress

The development of the railway train covers nearly two centuries. During that time, steam power has come and gone.

Electricity is now the standard energy supply for almost all locomotives, large and small. The electric power is supplied either from a third rail on the track or from overhead wires.

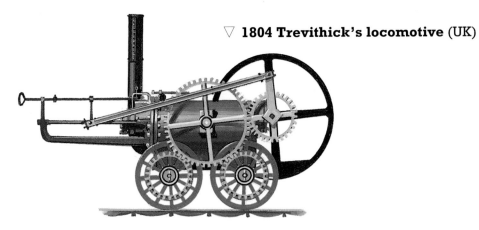

▽ **1804 Trevithick's locomotive** (UK)

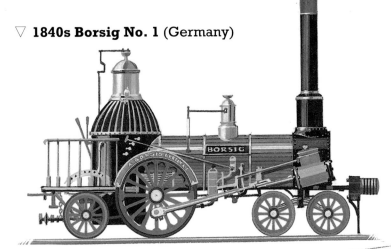

▽ **1840s Borsig No. 1** (Germany)

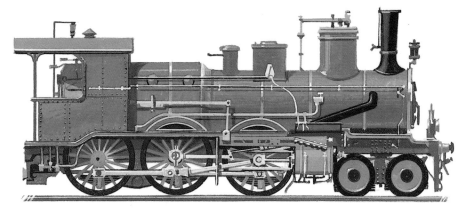

△ **1884 Vittorio-Emanuele II** (Italy)

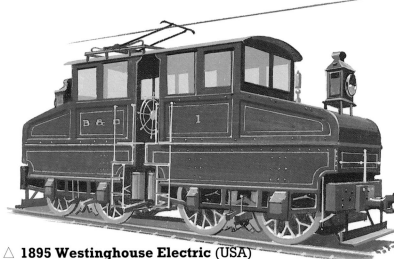

△ **1895 Westinghouse Electric** (USA)

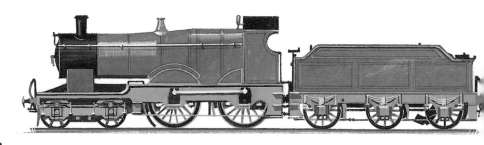

△ **1903 City of Truro** (UK)

27

▷ **1934 Burlington Zephyr** (USA)

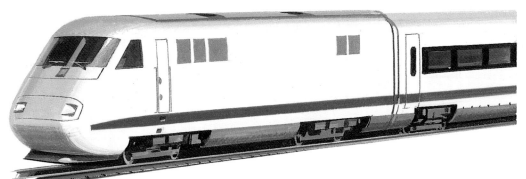

▽ **1938 Mallard** (UK)

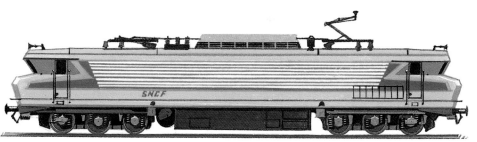

△ **1970s CC-21000** (France)

▷ **1990s ICE** (Germany)

Future rail

Rail travel of the future may be more like flying. The trains may float above the track, raised, or "levitated," into the air by magnetic forces. This system, called magnetic levitation – or "maglev" for short – has been tested in experimental trains. In the same way, they may "hang" from a monorail without touching it.

◁ This monorail carriage in Seattle has guide wheels to grip the side of the rail so that it does not fall over. Monorail trains run along a rail above or below them.

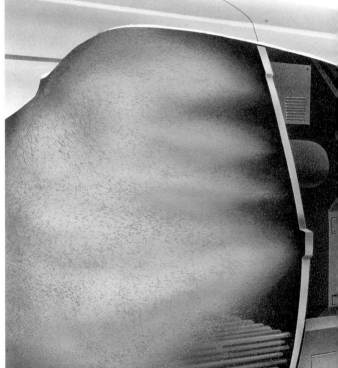

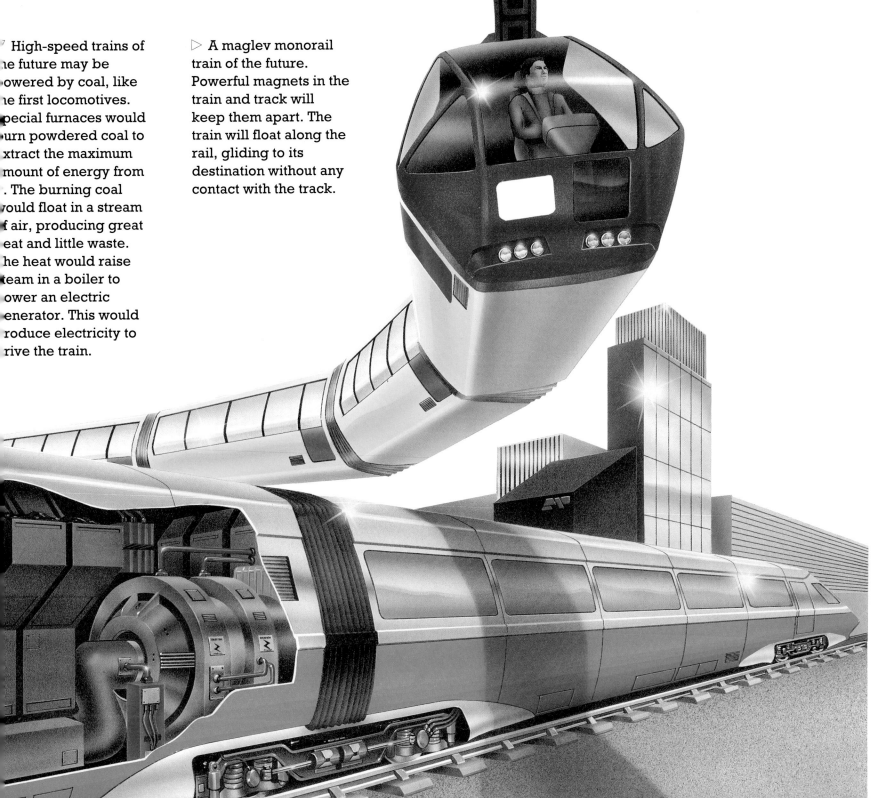

◁ High-speed trains of
the future may be
powered by coal, like
the first locomotives.
Special furnaces would
burn powdered coal to
extract the maximum
amount of energy from
it. The burning coal
would float in a stream
of air, producing great
heat and little waste.
The heat would raise
steam in a boiler to
power an electric
generator. This would
produce electricity to
drive the train.

▷ A maglev monorail
train of the future.
Powerful magnets in the
train and track will
keep them apart. The
train will float along the
rail, gliding to its
destination without any
contact with the track.

◁ An ocean liner off the coast of an island in the West Indies. When liners have to drop anchor away from the shore, passengers may be taken ashore by motor launch.

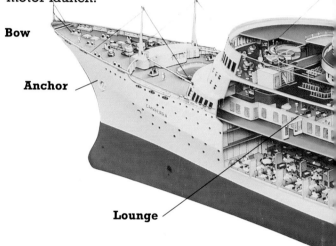

Bow

Anchor

Bridge, where officers keep watch and the ship is steered and navigated

Lounge

Hull, the body of the ship

Ocean liners take people on pleasure cruises. They are like floating hotels. People sleep in comfortable cabins and eat in large dining rooms. They can swim in pools or play games.

Liners stop at interesting places where the passengers may go on sight-seeing trips.

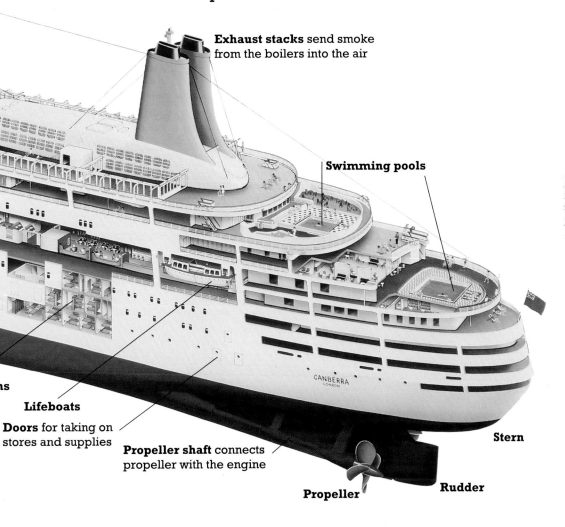

Mast for navigation lights and signal flag

Dance floor

Shops

Swimming pool

Exhaust stacks send smoke from the boilers into the air

Swimming pools

Offices

Stabilizers help to keep the ship steady for smooth cruising

Library

Cabins

Lifeboats

Doors for taking on stores and supplies

Propeller shaft connects propeller with the engine

Propeller

Rudder

Stern

CANBERRA
LONDON

Hovercraft

The hovercraft is a vehicle that travels on a layer of compressed air. It is also called an air-cushion vehicle (ACV). It can travel over land or water, floating just above the surface.

Hovercraft are used for carrying passengers and freight. Many car ferry services operate hovercraft.

▽ A hovercraft car ferry on the English Channel. The flexible "skirt" surrounding the lower edge of the craft is filled with air. This enables it to travel over uneven surfaces such as waves or rocks.

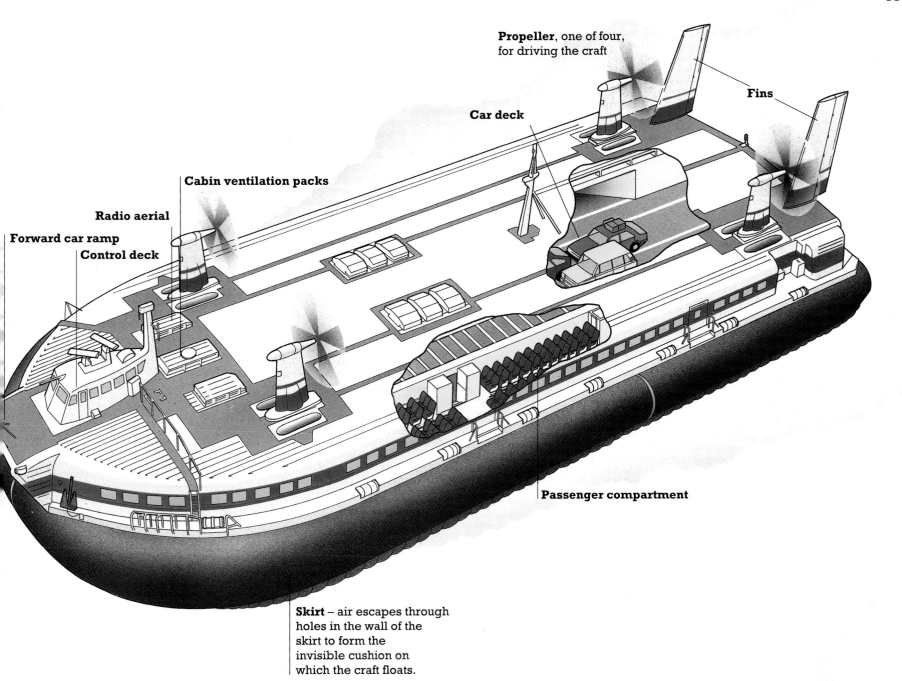

Propeller, one of four, for driving the craft

Fins

Car deck

Cabin ventilation packs

Radio aerial

Forward car ramp

Control deck

Passenger compartment

Skirt – air escapes through holes in the wall of the skirt to form the invisible cushion on which the craft floats.

Lifeboat

Lifeboats are craft used to rescue people in trouble at sea. There are lifeboat stations at intervals along the coast of many countries.

Different kinds of lifeboats are used, depending on the coastal conditions. Some lifeboats operate close to shore. Others may have to go far out to sea.

▽ The Tyne-class lifeboat is an ocean-going vessel with a crew of six and a top speed of 18 knots (21 mph or 33 km/h). If capsized, it rights itself in 5 seconds.

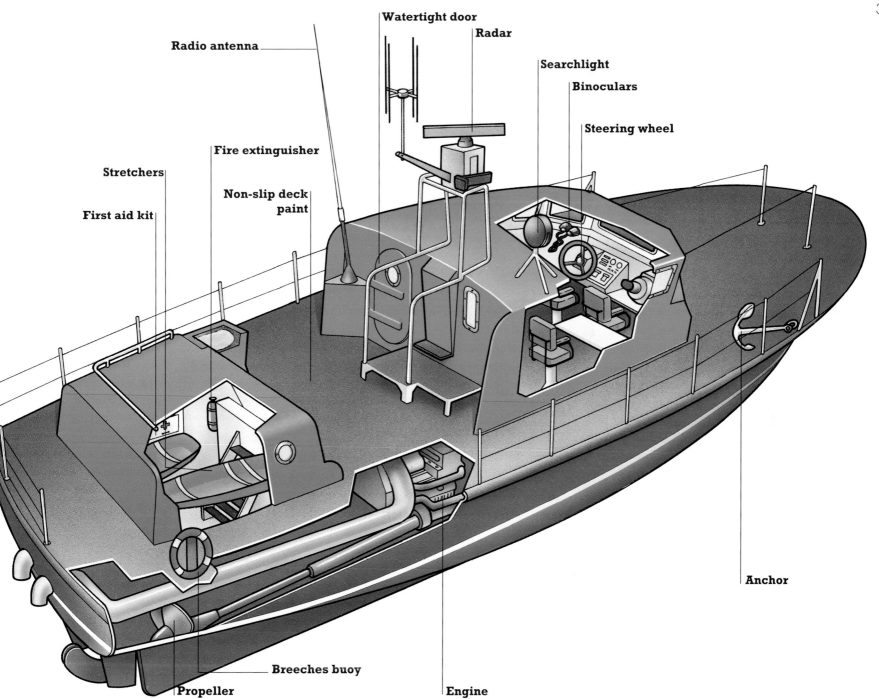

Radio antenna

Watertight door

Radar

Searchlight

Binoculars

Steering wheel

Fire extinguisher

Stretchers

Non-slip deck paint

First aid kit

Anchor

Breeches buoy

Propeller

Engine

Submersible

Submersibles are underwater craft. They are used for working or exploring underwater, or even for traveling to the bottom of the deepest oceans.

The pressure of water on humans and machines gets greater the farther down you go. Most manned submersibles have crew of two or three. But for deep-sea diving work, these are now being replaced with robot machines or by speci one-person diving suits.

◁ The one-person atmospheric diving system is now used for most deep-sea diving work. In this suit, called JIM, a diver can work at depths of more than 1,500 feet (450 m). The oil-filled arm and leg joints give the diver great freedom of movement, and a thruster pack at the back may be used for moving about. The suit keeps the diver at normal air pressure.

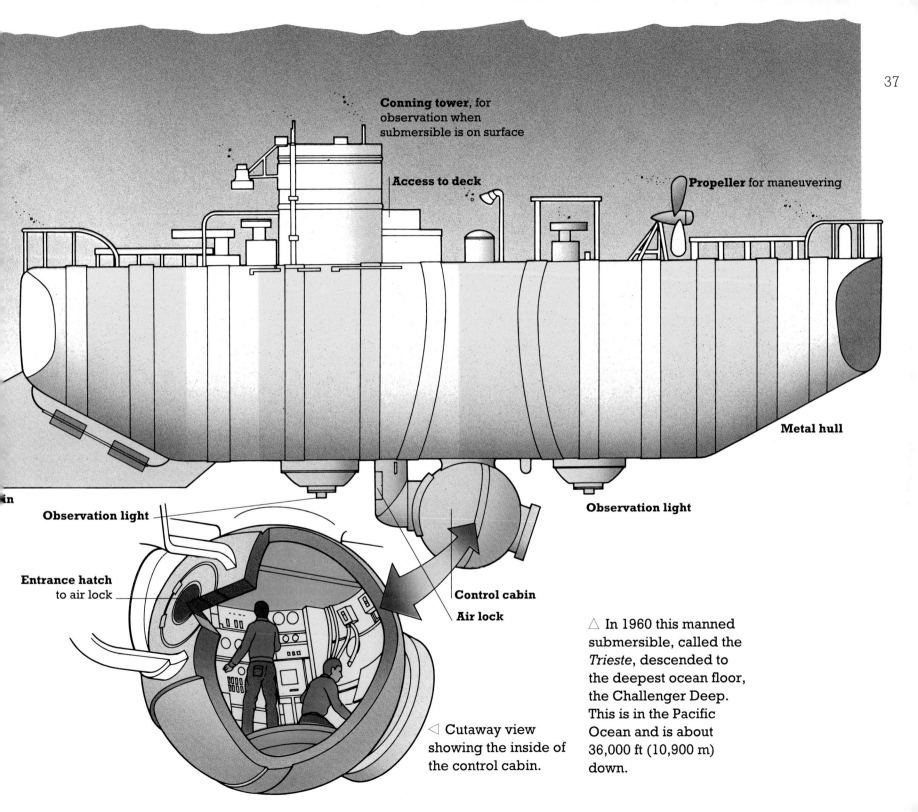

37

Conning tower, for observation when submersible is on surface

Access to deck

Propeller for maneuvering

Metal hull

Observation light

Observation light

Entrance hatch to air lock

Control cabin

Air lock

◁ Cutaway view showing the inside of the control cabin.

△ In 1960 this manned submersible, called the *Trieste*, descended to the deepest ocean floor, the Challenger Deep. This is in the Pacific Ocean and is about 36,000 ft (10,900 m) down.

Airliner

Airliners are the fastest means of transport in the world. Their routes crisscross the oceans and continents, linking airports in all parts of the globe.

The smallest airliners carry fewer than 10 passengers, the largest more than 500. Their speed ranges from that of a racing car to faster than a bullet from a gun.

◁ The Boeing 767 is a medium-haul, wide-body airliner that can seat more than 250 passengers. It has a cruising speed of 528 miles per hour (850 km/h) and a range of 2,554 miles (4,110 km)

Engine (turbofan

The airliner

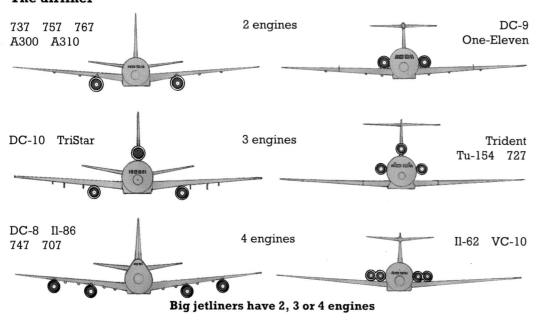

737 757 767 A300 A310	2 engines
	DC-9 One-Eleven
DC-10 TriStar	3 engines
	Trident Tu-154 727
DC-8 Il-86 747 707	4 engines
	Il-62 VC-10

Big jetliners have 2, 3 or 4 engines

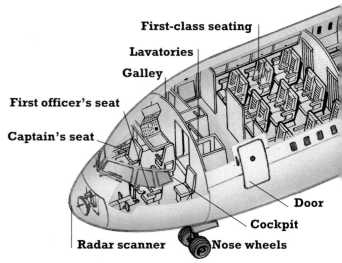

First-class seating
Lavatories
Galley
First officer's seat
Captain's seat
Door
Cockpit
Radar scanner
Nose wheels

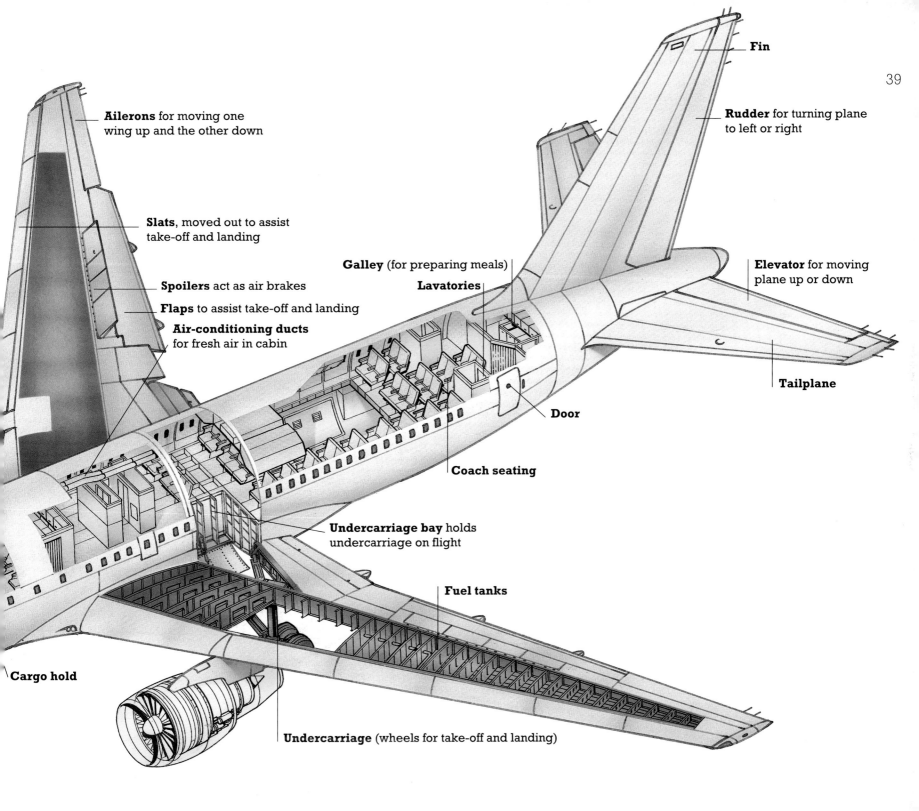

Ailerons for moving one wing up and the other down

Fin

Rudder for turning plane to left or right

Slats, moved out to assist take-off and landing

Galley (for preparing meals)

Lavatories

Elevator for moving plane up or down

Spoilers act as air brakes

Flaps to assist take-off and landing

Air-conditioning ducts for fresh air in cabin

Tailplane

Door

Coach seating

Undercarriage bay holds undercarriage on flight

Fuel tanks

Cargo hold

Undercarriage (wheels for take-off and landing)

Helicopter

Helicopters are flying machines with moving wings. The wings are called "rotors" because they go round in a circle
Rotors allow helicopters to take off and land straight up and down. Helicopters can also fly backward or sideways, and they can hover, staying in one spot in the air. These capabilities equip helicopters for special jobs such as emergency rescue.

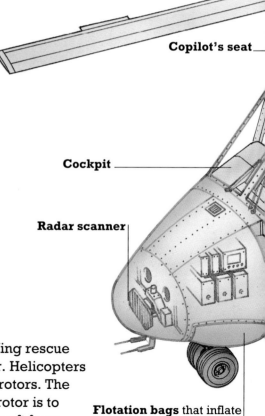

Copilot's seat

Cockpit

Radar scanner

◁ A Sea King rescue helicopter. Helicopters need two rotors. The small tail rotor is to keep the craft from spinning out of control.

Flotation bags that inflate in emergency landing on water

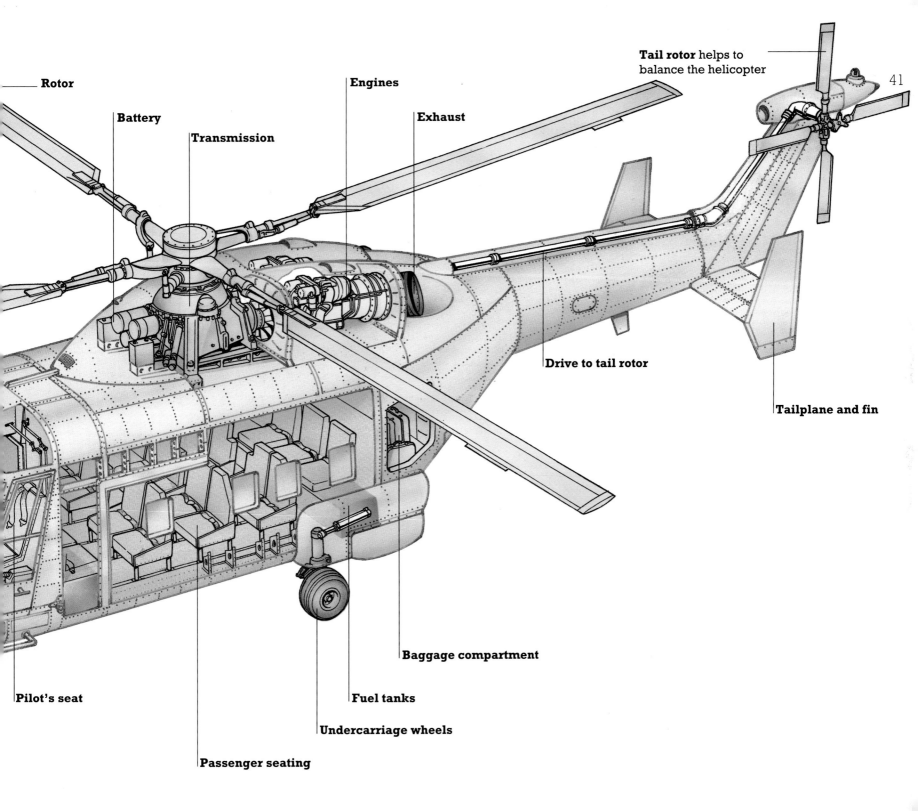

Rotor

Battery

Transmission

Engines

Exhaust

Tail rotor helps to
balance the helicopter

41

Drive to tail rotor

Tailplane and fin

Pilot's seat

Baggage compartment

Fuel tanks

Undercarriage wheels

Passenger seating

Helicopter jobs

Helicopters are versatile craft but they have three main drawbacks. They vibrate, they are noisy to fly and they are expensive to operate.

Even so, helicopters are ideal machines for short-haul or emergency work and other special jobs – much more efficient and adaptable than planes and other machines.

△ The MBB 105 (top), an emergency medical helicopter, and the MD 500, a tiny short-haul craft, are both equipped with undercarriage "skids" for landing on roug or uneven ground.

▽ The Bell 222 is a popular transport for businessmen in a hurry or for police work – crime prevention or traffic duty.

▷ The Kamov Ka-26 has "coaxial" rotors – one above the other. This Soviet chopper also has a circular antenna for use as a geological survey machine.

▽ The big twin-rotor Boeing 234 provides airline standards of comfort for its 44 passengers. It was developed from the CH-47 Chinook military heavy-lift helicopter.

HELIKOPTER SERVICE

▽ An Aérospatiale Dolphin used by the U.S. Coast Guard patrols off the Florida coast. Missions include anti-smuggling and rescue work.

COAST GUARD

△ Robinson claim their R22 is one of the cheapest two-seater helicopters available. This is a crop-sprayer version.

Strange transport machines

▽ The *14-bis* looked like a box kite. In 1906, its designer, Alberto Santos-Dumont, made the first official European heavier-than-air flights in it.

◁ The American Star of 1881 was an attempt to produce a safer bike than the standard penny-farthing, which had its large wheel at the front.

and tended to pitch forward down slopes. Less athletic people rode three- or even four-wheelers.

A modification of the penny-farthing was the American Star, which had the small wheel in front to stop it pitching down slopes.

High riders
In the early days of the bicycle, high-wheeled bikes became so common that they were known as "ordinaries." They had a large wheel in front, with a small wheel behind, and earned the nickname "penny-farthings." They were faster than the first bicycles, but were difficult to mount and ride,

△ Flying an autogyro, a "fun machine."

First flights
The early airplanes were curious machines. There were no rules to say where wings, engines, fins or rudders should be placed, or even how many there should be. The American brothers Wilbur and Orville Wright made the first successful flights in 1903, in *Flyer*, a twin-winged craft. Three years later, the *14-bis* made the first flight in Europe. Both these machines flew tail first and had their rudder at the front

Flying for fun
The autogyro is a flying machine that uses a propeller for power and a rotor to help it stay in the air. It cannot hover like a helicopter. Autogyros are mostly single-seaters and are flown for fun.

Tilt-rotor craft

Craft have been designed with helicopter rotors that tilt forward to serve as propellers in forward flight. The result is a flying machine with the lifting power of a helicopter and the speed and range of a plane.

Many of these advanced craft have now been developed, especially for military use. Bell helicopters did much experimental work, and a total of more than 600 of their V-22 Ospreys was planned. The need to cut defense spending in the United States halted production. But this unusual aircraft will no doubt emerge as a standard means of transport sometime in the future.

△ The experimental Bell 301 tilt-rotor craft with its rotors beginning to tilt forward. These are then used as propellers in fast forward flight.

△ Auto manufacturer Toyota holds an annual "Ideas Olympics," a competition that encourages weird and wonderful designs for cars. The design here, *Next Wheels*, was the 1989 winner.

A bicycle made for ten

As far back as the 19th century, an American bicycle was designed to seat 10 riders, one behind the other.

△ The Decemptuple, an American tandem built in 1896.

All kinds of power

◁ Hobby horses were bicycles without pedals. Special schools were set up to teach people how to ride these new machines in the early 1800s.

Muscle power

The modern bicycle is one of the most efficient ways of traveling by using muscle power. But the first bicycles did not have pedals. In the early 1800s, machines called velocipedes or hobby horses became popular. People who rode them had to push hard against the ground with their feet.

Many different kinds of power are used to drive transport machines, from muscle power to atomic energy. Animals have been used to draw carriages for thousands of years. Prehistoric people paddled canoes and sailed boats. Sailing makes use of the wind. People began to devise ways to make the most of human and animal effort – the invention of the wheel was probably the greatest advance in transport ever made. Since then, power sources for transport machines have included steam, electricity and gasoline.

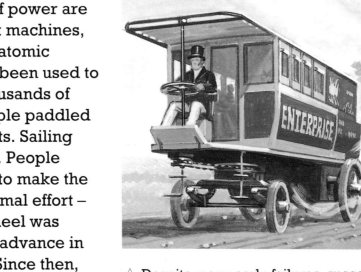

△ Despite many early failures, successful steam road vehicles were eventually built. In 1883, a steam carriage called *Enterprise* was carrying passengers around London.

△ One of today's most advanced trains, the French TGV runs on electric power from overhead lines.

Steam and electricity

Steam power never caught on for road vehicles, although there were some brief successes. Steam trains, however, from their development in the early 1800s, revolutionized transport in most parts of the world.

Steam is used to produce nearly two-thirds of the world's electric power. Fuel such as coal or oil is burned to heat water and produce steam to spin turbines, which in turn produce the electricity.

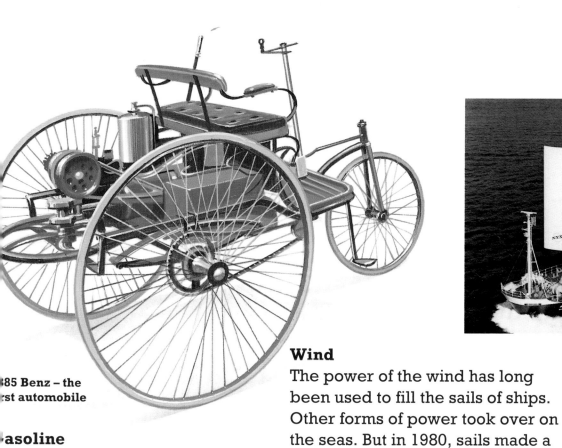

1885 Benz – the first automobile

Gasoline

Gasoline and other forms of refined petroleum oil are used to power most forms of road and air transport. It all began with the invention of the internal combustion engine in the 1850s. It was so called because the fuel – gas at first and then oil – was burned inside a chamber. The German engineer Gottlieb Daimler designed the first engine that could run on gasoline in 1883. Another German engineer, Karl Benz, mounted a gasoline engine on a tricycle in 1885 – the first ever automobile.

Wind

The power of the wind has long been used to fill the sails of ships. Other forms of power took over on the seas. But in 1980, sails made a comeback with a Japanese tanker that has sails made of steel and canvas. They are worked by computer, and are used to save fuel.

△ The *Shinaitoku Maru*, a "sailing" tanker. The sails are brought into use when the wind is right.

Solar power

The power of the sun is perhaps the fuel of the future. As a means of heating, it is already being used. But as a replacement for gasoline it is still only in its infancy.

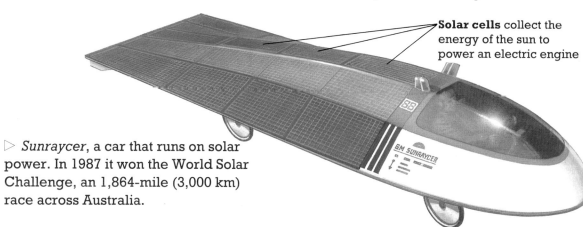

Solar cells collect the energy of the sun to power an electric engine

▷ *Sunraycer*, a car that runs on solar power. In 1987 it won the World Solar Challenge, an 1,864-mile (3,000 km) race across Australia.

Index